Old HUDDERSFIELD

by

Norman Ellis

C000130396

St. George's Square and the railway station, with horse drawn cabs and knickerbockered boys, probably 1906.

JUVAT IMPIGROS DEUS

HUDDERSFIELD.

Ja-Ja
REG^D
TRADEMARK.

HERALDIC SERIES.

© Norman Ellis 1994
First Published in the United Kingdom, 1994
By Richard Stenlake, Ochiltree Sawmill, The Lade,
Ochiltree, Ayrshire KA18 2NX
Telephone: 0290 700266

ISBN 1-872074-39-1

The coat of arms of the Borough of Huddersfield, reproduced opposite from the Ja-Ja series of heraldic postcards, was introduced in 1868. It slightly resembled the earlier Ramsden family arms. The towers, common on civic heraldry, were not specifically connected with Huddersfield's Tower Hill. The rams were a reminder of the town's link with textiles, particularly wool, although the topmost ram carried a sprig of cotton. The motto translated to 'God helps the diligent.'

INTRODUCTION

Mention Huddersfield; the famous choral society springs to mind; a link has always existed between hard environment and sturdy singing. Fresh upland air and an active life seemed to develop a desire to burst into song. The pursuit became supremely personified in the Huddersfield Choral Society, which adopted the Town Hall as its stamping ground. The Nonconformist chapels encouraged and nurtured the singing, but music was just as likely to be made in the open air at, say, Greenhead Park.

Huddersfield itself deserves some praise. Looked at impartially, the town may not readily commend itself. It has little stirring history and the present Parish Church in Kirkgate is deceptively 'new', having been built in 1834-6, admittedly on the site of an earlier church. The oldest structure in central Huddersfield is the Market Cross, erected shortly after John Ramsden was granted a charter in 1671 to hold a weekly market there.

The town is markedly made up of grid-patterned wide streets with storeyed stone buildings. The gems are abundant; dominant ones grab you, for example the railway station or the beautifully restored Victorian Market. The parallelism and spaciousness of the streets was a deliberate attempt by the Ramsdens, from mid 19th century onwards, to create a town *par excellence* to replace the earlier unpretentious one.

It is impossible to consider Huddersfield without reference to the Ramsden family. Queen Elizabeth sold the Manor of Huddersfield to William Ramsden in 1599 for £965-10s-9d. In 1920, Huddersfield Corporation purchased the estate, which included most of the town centre, from the sixth baronet, Sir John Frencheville Ramsden.

In 1766, Sir John Ramsden built the Cloth Hall in Market Street, where local weavers could display their wares. By late 19th century, many manufacturers preferred to display their cloth in town warehouses and the Cloth Hall was demolished in 1930. Sir John also constructed the Huddersfield Broad Canal and was partly responsible for the Huddersfield Narrow Canal. The later Ramsdens had a policy of prohibiting back-to-back houses on their land.

Domestic spinning and weaving, undertaken by families in their cottages, were the prologue to Huddersfield's development as a textile centre. Much of the industry became concentrated near the river and canal, where water was available for power, processing, transport and waste disposal. The large mills produced woollen, worsted and some cotton goods. Huddersfield worsted, with its wide range of designs and colours, became internationally famous.

Complementing the textile industry were engineering and machinery making concerns. But after textiles, Huddersfield's next important industry was chemicals, particularly dyestuffs. A century and a half ago, Mr. Read Holliday realised that coal tar, then considered a useless incidental of gas production, offered seemingly untold possibilities. From the first sheds which Holliday built, the huge ICI complex evolved. A chemist called Mansfield, who worked in the town, pronounced that bread and butter would one day be made from coal tar!

Huddersfield became a municipal borough in 1868, a county borough in 1888, and in 1974 it was chosen as administrative centre of Kirklees Metropolitan Council. A measure of the town's growth is the increase of population from 7000 in1801 to 95,000 in 1901. Huddersfield, even with some capitulation to modernisation, remains as a significant affirmation of 19th century prosperity.

Norman Ellis, July 1994.

Huddersfield Market Place early this century. The Jubilee Fountain, centre, was unveiled in 1888. Freeman, Hardy & Willis, multiple-store boot and shoe makers, sold their products here at 7 Market Place, also at 23 Cross Church Street and 65 New Street. Jones' Sewing Machines, at 9 Market Place, later transferred to Kirkgate and the Market Hall. In Kirkgate (left) are two typically Victorian buildings dating from 1879, one housing the Waverley Hotel.

Market Place in 1923. The market cross (almost obscuring the fountain, right of centre) was erected shortly after the granting of market rights in 1671. Following removal to Longley Hall for several decades, it was re-erected in the Market Place in 1852. The Market Place used to accommodate the Tuesday market and provide a site for orators and mass meetings, but for well over a century has been such in name only.

NEW ST. HUDD?

Broad and level, Huddersfield's New Street became a popular shopping area, although an air of tranquility pervades this Edwardian view. Were the three men, including a policeman, posing for the camera? Above the Hey & Co. hosiery shop, at the corner with King Street, was the Jennings' Business Training College which offered 'Daily training to young ladies and gentlemen in subjects of practical value, such as arithmetic, book-keeping, shorthand, typewriting, spelling, grammar, letter writing etc.'

NEW STREET HUDD. (135.)

Prominent on this view of New Street, circa 1905, are the Huddersfield Banking Company premises of 1881, with their onion shaped dome. Most of this now-demolished building faced on to Cloth Hall Street. Opposite, horse drawn carts and a tram are about to vie for space in King Street. Throughout this century, numerous changes in appearance and tenancy of shop buildings in New Street have occurred. In 1905, the Cash Supply Stores, at no.33, sold Fife Whisky at 3-6d per bottle, Force at 6d per packet and Payton's Wallpaper Cleaner at $10^{1}/2$d for a 1-0d tin.

NEW ST. HUDDERSFIELD. 396.

A later view of New Street. The large light-coloured building, centre right, was at the time tenanted by Montague Burton, but subsequently became a Marks & Spencer store. To its right were Dr. Scholls, True-Form and Stylo, the latter in the Tudor House. The rest of Tudor House had Dunns the hatters, at no.33, with double awning. Nearer the camera were Alexandre ladies and gents tailors (Why pay more?) and Collinsons the confectioners.

NEW STREET, HUDDERSFIELD.

5946

A more recent view of New Street when trams had been replaced by trolleybuses, one of which is just visible. Discernible on the left, in addition to Taylors chemists, are the shops of two furnishers, James Woodhouse & Son and Sykes & Co., also two clothiers, Hepworth & Son and Fifty Shilling Tailors, whose premises stretched round into Cloth Hall Street.

The Neoclassical style facade of Huddersfield's railway station, shown above, is one of the finest in England. The station was built in 1846-50 for the Huddersfield & Manchester (later London & North Western) and Lancashire & Yorkshire Railways. The central building, originally a hotel, was given a pedimented portico with Corinthian columns. The long arcaded sections on either side were flanked by pavilions (not shown) which initially served as booking halls for the respective railway companies. Trams competed with trains for shorter journeys; the foremost charabanc was, however, advertising a trip to Southport.

10

RAILWAY STATION, Interior, HUDDERSFIELD (145 B⁄?)

Until 1886, Huddersfield Station had one main platform which incorporated a pair of bay platforms. The large island platform was then added, connected by a subway, thus providing two more main and three more bay platforms. Some of the bays, including the one with the L & Y locomotive, above, are no longer in use and the signal cabin, left, has gone. The original platform, which was behind the station facade, is on the right. To the west of the station, partly visible left, were goods sheds and sidings.

PHOTO. H. LUMB.
COWCLIFFE.

CONSTRUCTION OF THE MIDLAND LINE,
OCT 31st 1908,
HILLHOUSE.

Huddersfield almost had a second railway station – at Newtown – not far from its main station. The Midland Railway, which conceived the idea, laid track from Mirfield to Newtown, running close and parallel to the existing L & NW line. The above photo shows construction at Hillhouse, north of Newtown, with manual labour, horse power, some mechanisation – and inherent problems. The line opened for goods traffic in 1910, but the passenger station and a railway hotel were never built. Parts of the branch were in use until 1968.

St. George's Square,
Huddersfield.

Spacious St. George's Square, when private cars were in the ascendant and were parked indiscriminately beside the statue of Sir Robert Peel. The statue, unveiled in 1873, was removed in 1949. The lion is prominent atop the Lion Building of 1852-4. On the right are the Britannia Buildings, erected in 1856-9, but showing a later ground floor 'modern' interpolation of the Huddersfield Building Society.

JOHN WILLIAM ST. HUDDERSFIELD. 403.

John William Street at its junction with Westgate, left, and Kirkgate, when traffic must have warranted use of a point-duty policeman. The street was named after Sir John William Ramsden. The departmental store on the left belonged to the long-established Rushworths. Nos. 2-4 John William Street, right, had been taken by Montague Burton, described as 'the largest merchant tailoring organisation in the world'. Their other Huddersfield shops were at 19-23 New Street, 14 and 39 King Street and 46 Cross Church Street. The Burton organisation, which started in Leeds in 1900, was acclaimed for a caring attitude towards its workers.

Huddersfield YMCA was founded in a cellar in 1911. It later moved to these commodious premises at 16 John William Street, which had been refurbished by Lunn & Cardno, decorators, Manchester Street. In 1957, the YMCA moved to the former Primitive Methodist Church in Northumberland Street. By then, it had opened other clubs in surrounding areas. The shops shown were, left to right, a mantle warehouse, booksellers and boot/shoe retailers.

THIS IS A REAL PHOTO

QUEEN STREET, HUDDERSFIELD.

462 / 25

Cross Church Street viewed from Queen Street, circa 1912. St. Peter's Parish Church, of Norman foundation, was built last century in a 15th century style. Hiltons, who were well-known in several West Riding towns, sold boots and shoes from their shop at the corner with King Street. Netherwoods were tailors and clothiers.

16

King Street at its junction with Queen Street, and Cross Church Street. Omens of the future were the traffic lights and one-way street sign. The Netherwood shop at 39 King Street had become part of the Burton empire, but Hiltons still occupied the opposite corner. George Hall Ltd., drapers, were expanding and had branched into carpets. Their other premises were in Cloth Hall Street. George Frederick Bradley, jeweller and watchmaker, traded in the block used by Halls. Further up, beneath the clock, was the much-loved indoor market, demolished in 1970.

Victorian elegance in Westgate, Huddersfield, circa 1903. Buildings such as these usually had office and warehouse accommodation on the higher floors, although most of the income came from shop lettings at ground level. Some shops also used basements and cellars. Cooper & Webb were grocers and provision merchants; also railway and shipping agents.

18

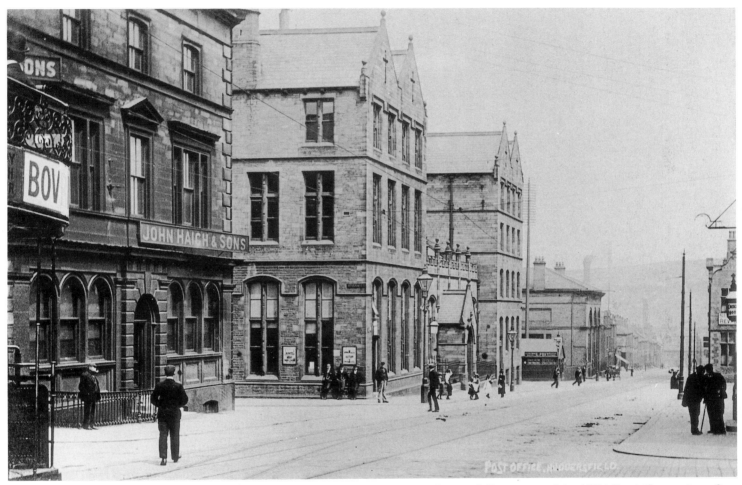

Northumberland Street very early this century, with the old General Post Office, erected in 1874-5, at the centre of the picture. In 1900, its staff consisted of a postmaster, 54 officers and clerks, 100 inspectors and letter carriers, 9 telegraphists and 37 boy messengers. Nearer the camera are premises of John Haigh & Sons, woollen and worsted manufacturers. The small building beyond the GPO housed G. Fox, picture frame maker. A tramcar is partly visible, left, with a Bovril advert.

The Royal Mail Parcel Coach outside Huddersfield General Post Office in 1904. It plied between Huddersfield and Leeds via Halifax and Bradford.

'Sacked' Post Office workers. A light moment in front of Huddersfield G.P.O.

NORTHUMBERLAND ST. HUDDERSFIELD. 106.

The Princess Cinema was opened on Whit Saturday 19th May 1923, by Miss Peggy Hyland, film star. It was built within the shell of a warehouse (visible on page 19) then occupied by Herbert Dickinson, woollen merchant. The warehouse was purchased for £8,000; alterations, including construction of a new steel frame within the walls, cost £34,000. The first public film, a silent called *Way Down East* starring Lilian Gish, was shown from Monday 21st May. The basement Café Dansant was completed shortly after.

HUDDERSFIELD'S FIRST WATERWORKS, OLD WELLS FOUND IN THE MARKET PLACE MARCH 3ᴿᴰ 06.

During excavations in the Market Place for underground conveniences in March 1906, two large arched-over tanks were discovered. They were the remains of an abortive attempt early in the previous century to supply water to the town from nearby Bradley Spout, via the tanks, and four pumps, one at each corner of the Market Place. Someone, it seems, failed to take full account of water's reluctance to flow uphill.

RED DOOR STORES, PACK HORSE YARD.

BEST VALUE IN YORKSHIRE

Our Stock :
70,000 TILES from 1d. each.

LAWN MOWERS, 14/6.

BARROWS, 14/6.

Garden Rollers, &c.
Winter Stoves from 8/6.

—::—

Second-hand FURNITURE.

FRESH ARRIVALS DAILY.

—::—

LARGE STOCK OF
Oil Paintings, Water Colours,
Engravings, &c.

Telephone
22 x.

Established
1888.

D. McCLELLAN & COMPANY, PROPRIETORS.

Pack Horse Yard, so called because it originally incorporated stabling for packhorses, was entered from either King Street or Kirkgate. The latter entry was between the Pack Horse and White Swan Hotels, almost opposite the Parish Church. The first Huddersfield Dispensary was established there in 1814. Shops were later established in the yard, including McClellan's Red Door Stores, whose advert from early this century is pictured. Pack Horse Yard was demolished in 1966 to make way for a shopping precinct.

Joe Riley was a well-known wholesale and retail cigar merchant and tobacco blender in Huddersfield. Established in 1864, he eventually had three shops in the town, including one in Brook's Yard, off Market Street, very probably that pictured above about 1910. Tobacco mixtures then cost around 5d per ounce and good cigars 5 for a shilling.

Looking down Springdale Street in Rashcliffe, a working-class mill suburb to the southwest of Huddersfield. The small front gardens, ample roadway and wide pavements provided a stylish air. This card was used for a Christmas greeting in 1904. All the houses are still there, little altered externally.

Looking down Thornton Lodge Road, also in Rashcliffe. It runs parallel to Springdale Street. In the distance, part of Paddock Viaduct is visible. Leading off at left are Crosland Road (nearest camera) and Moor Bottom Road. A block of shops, including Kashmir Stores, now adjoins the gable end (behind the carter). The horse and cart belonged to H.J. Purkis, wholesale and retail butcher, of 20 Cross Church Street, Huddersfield.

MOLDGREEN
HUDDERSFIELD

Moldgreen, a suburb of Huddersfield, looking north early this century. Shops are visible, as is the large Classical styled United Methodist Free Church on Chapel Street, demolished in 1989. This and a Church of England, a Congregational and a Wesleyan Methodist Church supplied the community's spiritual needs. The area, largely working-class, benefited from the coming of the trams in the 1880s, which traversed Wakefield Road, shown near the base of the picture. Their advent led to further housing development, some of it inferior.

FARTOWN GREEN

Fartown Green Road, looking towards Fartown Green, and Pollard Street intersecting at right and left, where the workshop of Tom Stansfield, village bootmaker, is visible. Most of the neat houses and their decorative chimney pots are still there today. The wrought iron railings, gas lamps and meditative people convey an air of Edwardian elegance. In reality, life for most people was arduous.

29

In 1883, Huddersfield became the first municipal tramway operator in Britain. The trams were steam propelled, each double-deck trailer car being pulled by a steam locomotive. The last steam tram ran in 1902. Operation by electric traction commenced in 1901; the first batch of electric tramcars were numbered 1-25, of which no.4 is shown. The lower saloon seated 24 on longitudinal upholstered seats; the upper deck had seating for 32 on transverse wooden seats. The location is Spaines Road, Fartown; the houses still stand.

Left: The Huddersfield tramway system was progressive and well maintained, with eventual standardisation of vehicles. In the early days, experimentation and modification were common. No. 76 was a unique example. It was delivered in 1910 from makers United Electric Car Co. of Preston for alterations: the open upper-deck balconies were enclosed, nearside front exits added at each end, folding platform doors fitted, glass screens placed behind the driver, and reversed stairs incorporated. But the driver, or motorman, was still exposed to the weather.

Right: No. 93, captured in Ray Street with the railway viaduct behind, was part of a batch of ten trams purchased in 1913. Their folding platform doors and enclosed vestibules gave the driver protection. The open balconies each had a double forward-facing seat, popular with passengers in fine weather and small boys at any time. Huddersfield's last new tramcars were eight superb all-enclosed vehicles built in 1931-2. They were sold to Sunderland Corporation in 1938. Tramway operation in Huddersfield ended in 1940.

The Coronation of King George V and Queen Mary in June 1911 was celebrated by running the above tramcar, believed to be no.3, decorated in red, white and blue and carrying over 1500 lamps. Here it is posed in Ray Street, near Great Northern Street Depot. The opposite side of the car carried the words, 'Long live the Queen'.

Trolleybuses were introduced to Huddersfield in 1933. They were big six-wheelers, capable of matching the high seating capacity of the town's modern trams. When the trolleybus system was about to close, no.623 was specially adorned. It is pictured in Kirkgate on its final journey to Waterloo on the last day of trolleybus operation, 13th July 1968.

J. S. GIBSON, PURVEYOR IN TRIPE, &c.

PURE BEEF DRIPPING REFINER. (Wholesale and Retail).

Works:

St. Andrew's Road.

TELEPHONE 129[Y.

Branches:

49, Northgate

18 & 23, Beast Market

29, Market Street, Paddock

57, Colne Road

58, Lidget Street, Lindley

77, Leeds Road

—:o:—

Hotels and Restaurants :: :: catered for on Reasonable Terms.

—:o:—

GUARANTEED RELIABLE AND FRESH SUPPLIES DAILY.

Tripe has long been associated with the West Riding. The cow's stomach provided seam, honeycomb and 'dark'. From the udder came elder. Specialist tripe dressers prepared the tripe and delivered it to shops or sold it on market stalls. Seasoned with salt, vinegar and possibly pepper, it provided a cheap and tasty meal. Umpteen recipes existed for cooking tripe, including tripe-and-onions. Tripe dressers also handled cow heels and often doubled as dripping refiners. Well-known in Huddersfield was the firm of J.S. Gibson, whose works were in St. Andrew's Road.

34

Early this century, Joe Andrew was a tripe dresser and dripping refiner in St. Andrew's Road. By about 1916, he had moved to Beaumont Street, near the slaughter house, where the above photograph was probably taken sometime later.

Daniel Wainwright was a Huddersfield removal contractor and horse dealer with addresses at Bradford Road, Viaduct Street and St. Andrew's Road earlier this century. This cart or rulley, with a shire horse in harness, was decorated in aid of sick and wounded horses. In the background are two furniture removal vans.

Sale of Carting Plant at Pickfords Stables Huddersfield for D. Wainwright. by M Scorah Auctioneer

Around 1909, Pickford & Co., carriers, had a depot at the railway station, with horse stabling in nearby Viaduct Street, where the above sale of carting plant and horses for Daniel Wainwright (previous page) was held. Here a shire is being put through its paces on spare ground in front of the tramway shed in Great Northern Street, near Viaduct Street. The location can be pinpointed by Beaumont Street School, left, built in 1874, and demolished in early 1994 after a fire.

Medals, shields and a cup extol the achievements of boy swimmers at the Parish Church School, situated in the lower part of Kirkgate. It is likely they swam at nearby Ramsden Street Baths, which opened in 1879 and closed in 1972.

Huddersfield Royal Infirmary was built in 1829-31. Its splendid facade, with four-column Grecian Doric portico, overlooked New North Road. The Infirmary replaced the Dispensary which had been set up in a former house in Pack Horse Yard. The Dispensary only provided for outpatients, a function which it continued after the Infirmary opened. The facade of the Infirmary is shown above in about 1910. A notice board, right, lists its bathing facilities. The baths, which were opened each day except Sunday from 10.00 a.m. onwards, included Russian, Turkish, medicated and slipper bathing from 6d to 2-6d per head. Separate periods were allocated for ladies and gentlemen.

WARD 4. ROYAL INFIRMARY, HUDDERSFIELD. (140M)

Ward 4 of Huddersfield Royal Infirmary, same period as previous view. In Edwardian times, most homes had a box of liquid or powder home cures. In 1905, Henry Sykes, a chemist in Pack Horse Yard produced Sykes's Spring and Autumn Medicine for the blood and skin at 7½d or 1-0d a box. Working class people reluctantly resorted to the doctor because of his inevitable bill. Occurrence of many diseases which are unfamiliar today, plus industrial injuries, placed heavy demand upon the Infirmary. Those admitted received skilled but disciplined treatment.

40

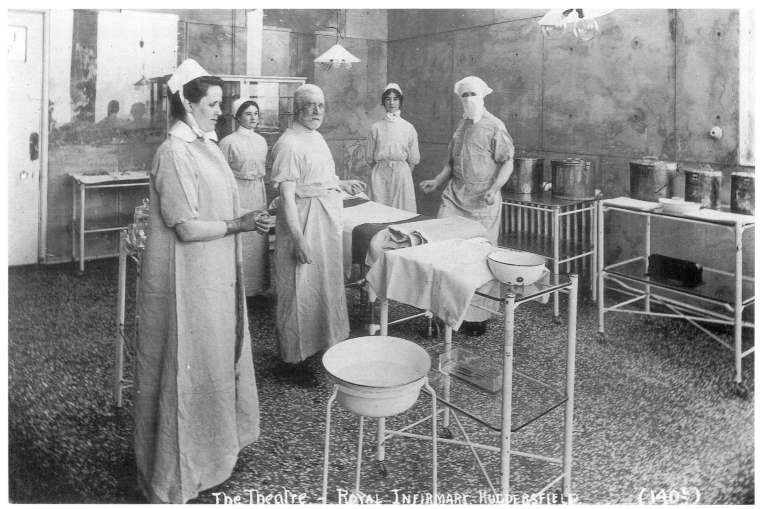

The Theatre - Royal Infirmary Huddersfield (1905)

Operating theatre. Surgery was a last resort, but often necessary after industrial injury. Some workers subscribed to friendly societies, which paid out limited amounts towards medical treatment or unemployment benefit. The Infirmary was run as a medical charity; it relied heavily on benefactors or subscribers for funds. Some local employers channelled money to the Infirmary in expectation of having employees treated and quickly returned to work.

This event was held on a Sunday afternoon in fine weather and attracted a large crowd. The vocalists and instrumentalists rendered items from *Messiah* and led the hymn singing. The Rev. J.F. Porteous, Baptist minister, seen above left, and Mr. James Haigh, president of the event, gave addresses. The £22.7s taken at the gates and in the enclosure went to Huddersfield Infirmary and the Victoria Sick Poor Nurses' Association.

Competing with the Church of England, and often with each other, were Huddersfield's various Nonconformist denominations, which were generally well supported by textile workers, tradesmen, manufacturers, and their families. Nonconformist buildings were of varied design, dimensions and architectural merit.

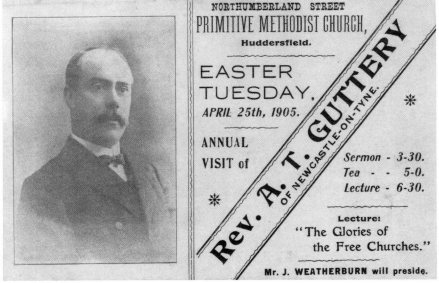

Highfield Congregational Church, off New North Road, centre of lower picture, c.1905, was built in 1843-4. Behind its fine Classical facade was an impressive galleried interior, with total seating for around 900. The Sunday School is shown to the right.

NORTHUMBERLAND STREET
PRIMITIVE METHODIST CHURCH,
Huddersfield.

EASTER TUESDAY,
APRIL 25th, 1905.

ANNUAL VISIT of

Rev. A. T. GUTTERY
OF NEWCASTLE-ON-TYNE.

Sermon - 3-30.
Tea - - 5-0.
Lecture - 6-30.

Lecture:
"The Glories of the Free Churches."

Mr. J. WEATHERBURN will preside.

In and around Huddersfield, the Primitive Methodists were less well represented than the Wesleyans and some other Methodist branches. Their central church was in Northumberland Street. Nonconformists were great champions of preaching, singing and get-togethers, as the advertisement card for the Northumberland Street 'Prims' signifies.

360 IN GREENHEAD PARK. HUDDERSFIELD.

Acquisition of a public park near the centre of Huddersfield was debated for many years. On 3rd July 1869, the Greenhead site was thrown open for three hours and visited by several thousand people (after the fields had been newly mown). The site was eventually purchased by public subscription from Sir John William Ramsden for £25,000 and opened to the public in 1884. Its amenities subsequently included terraced gardens, shrubberies, flower beds, pools, a bandstand, playing fields, bowling greens, tennis courts and putting greens. Messing about with small boats was obviously popular.

Greenhead Park accommodated all kinds of events. The third annual exhibition of Huddersfield Floral & Horticultural Society was held there on 7th-8th August 1908. During the event, its Committee of Management posed in the park for the above photo. The exhibition was opened by Lady Francesse Legge of Woodsome Hall. There were numerous classes for plants, fruit, vegetables and cut blooms, also special classes for schools. Tradesmen's turnouts, daylight fireworks and illuminations were amongst the many other attractions.

Robert Airey & Son were coopers at Chapel Hill Mills, East Parade. Their workforce pose in front of a large wooden cask early this century. Who was the rose amongst the thorns?

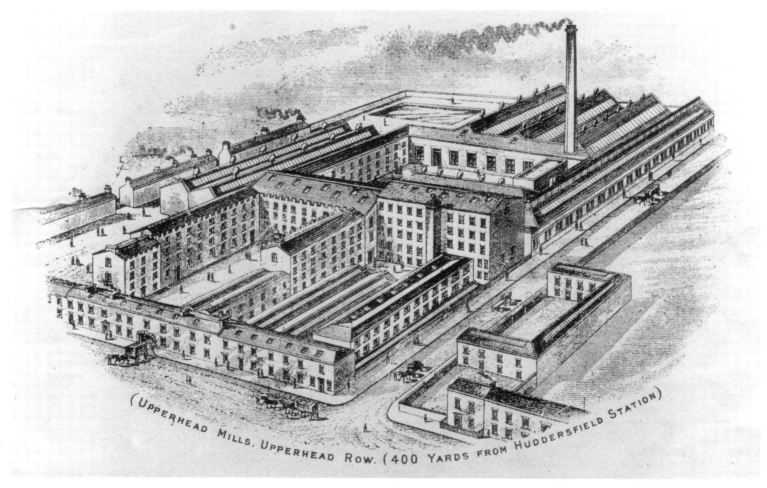

(UPPERHEAD MILLS, UPPERHEAD ROW. (400 YARDS FROM HUDDERSFIELD STATION)

Lockwood & Keighley Ltd. was established in 1798 by Joshua Lockwood. The large complex is depicted above around 1900, with Upperhead Row in the foreground and Henry Street running diagonally right. The various mill buildings accommodated a succession of processes, including weaving, dyeing and finishing. Workers' houses and the mill reservoir are also visible. The firm produced high quality cloths for mens' garments such as whipcords, Bedford cords and riding tweeds and received many English and overseas awards.

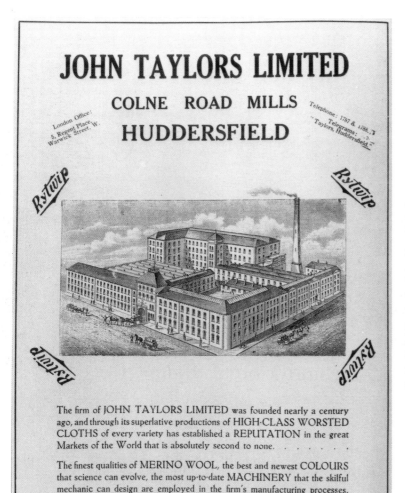

JOHN TAYLORS LIMITED

COLNE ROAD MILLS

London Office:
5, Regent Place,
Warwick Street, W.

Telephone: 1787 & 1788.
Telegrams:
"Taylors, Huddersfield."

HUDDERSFIELD

Rytwip

The firm of JOHN TAYLORS LIMITED was founded nearly a century ago, and through its superlative productions of HIGH-CLASS WORSTED CLOTHS of every variety has established a REPUTATION in the great Markets of the World that is absolutely second to none. . . . . .

The finest qualities of MERINO WOOL, the best and newest COLOURS that science can evolve, the most up-to-date MACHINERY that the skilful mechanic can design are employed in the firm's manufacturing processes. The IDEAL aimed at throughout all its departments is to provide the High-Class Buying Public with CLOTHS that will stand the test of wear and will meet the specific needs of the most exacting critic. . . . . .

The mills shown in this 1917 advert were built by brothers Henry Dyson Taylor and John William Taylor in 1856. Colne Road is in the foreground; Queen Street South on the right. *Rytwip* was the company's registered name for whipcords and gabardines. *Coromil* and *Kooltex* were its trademarks for worsted suitings and tropical suitings respectively. Spinning, weaving and dyeing were carried out at the Colne Road Mills. To provide healthy happy working conditions, a canteen (opened in 1916), recreation room (with table tennis tables) and free chiropody service were introduced.

John Taylors Limited celebrated its centenary in 1956 when the above photographs were released. *Left:* the mending room, with good seating and lighting for the young ladies. Even when using modern equipment, mending of fabric which became damaged at the weaving or later stages was desirable. *Right:* the pattern department.

This fire, at the mill of Richard Mellor & Co., worsted cloth manufacturers, Firth Street, Huddersfield, was reported by Mr. Parkinson, a tripe dresser. It was attended by the corporation hose cart, seen above, and steam fire engine, both horse drawn, which were under jurisdiction of the police. At its height, nine jets were directed on to the blaze. Damage to the building, which contained looms, yarn and cloth, was severe, and later estimated at over £6,000, although a nearby shed of looms was saved. After the fire, Police Fireman Darlington fell from a fire escape whilst retrieving a hose pipe and was diagnosed as having a fractured skull.

Read Holliday & Sons Ltd. was founded in 1830 by Mr. Read Holliday, whose family were wool spinners and flour millers in the Bradford area. Aged 21, using waste products from the gasworks, he started to distil ammonia (which was used for wool scouring) in premises at Tanfield, off Leeds Road. Following complaints about pollution from his works, Read Holliday moved in 1839 to a site at Turnbridge, near the Huddersfield Gas Light Company premises on the eastern flank of the town. Coal tar, then considered a useless by-product of gas production, was there distilled into a range of products. Read Holliday and his five sons developed a huge chemical complex at Turnbridge. It is shown above in 1914, looking towards Huddersfield.

New Offices and Warehouses, Huddersfield.

Old Warehouse and Offices, Upperhead Row, Huddersfield.

Apart from its famous colour dyes, Read Holliday's list of products included washing powders, soaps, disinfectants, coal briquettes, creosote for railway sleepers, and naptha for lamps. The company branched into manufacture of dyeing and related machines for the textile industry. It spread to other parts of the country and abroad. But from the end of the last century, it suffered from severe competition. To improve efficiency, new offices and warehouses were opened in St. Andrew's Road, Turnbridge, in 1914, replacing those in Upperhead Row in the town centre. Each of these is shown above. The new buildings are also visible in the photo on the previous page, right of centre distance.

A 2 HORSE LURRY.

A MOTOR LURRY.

READ HOLLIDAY & SONS LTD

ANILINE DYE MANUFACTURERS HUDDERSFIELD

A RAILWAY TANK WAGGON.

The firm of Read Holliday sunk collieries to provide coal for its steam boilers. It had a wharf on the adjacent canal from where its barges carried goods to Goole, Hull, Manchester and Liverpool. Some of its other transport is shown here; the road vehicles were photographed outside the new offices and warehouses in St. Andrew's Road. Modernisation apart, by 1914 the workforce had been reduced to 750, having once stood at 1500. The war brought government intervention. The company became part of British Dyes Ltd., which later formed a constituent of Imperial Chemical Industries at a new complex at Dalton.

A solid-tyred motor lorry of Richard Henry Inman, mineral water manufacturer, at his works in Firth Street. The Karrier chassis had just been bodied at the works of T.J. Constantine in Hipperholme, and given a Huddersfield registration.

Mobile ice cream shop of Antonio Coletta & Sons, wholesale and retail ice cream producers, parked at their Hebble Bridge Works in Bradford Road, Huddersfield. This type of vehicle, popular from the late 1920s, carried a large cylindrical ice-insulated container from which ice cream was scooped. It tasted good in the cornets, wafers (sandwiches), shells or cardboard tubs.

1912 · Huddersfield Northern Union F.C. · 1913.

A. Bennett. Trainer

D. Clark.

John Clifford. Vice-President
W. Trevarthen
E. Wrigley.
YORKS. CHALLENGE CUP.

R. Lockwood. Committee
J. W. Higson.
S. Moorhouse.
A. Rosenfeld.

Joe Clifford. Chairman
B. Gronow
H. Wagstaff, (CAPT.)
YORKS. LEAGUE CUP.

H. Lodge. Committee
F. Longstaff
J. Davies.

W. Brook.
T. H. Grey.
M. Holland.

M. Sutcliffe. Committee
H. Sherwood.
W. F. Kitchen.
NORTHERN LEAGUE CUP.

H. Bennett. Under-Trainer
H. Walton.

Chas. Sykes. President

Huddersfield was amongst the first twenty clubs to join the Northern Union, formed out of a breakaway from the English Rugby Union in 1895. Huddersfield fared badly until after Harold Wagstaff of Underbank, Holmfirth, joined in 1906. From the 1911-12 season, he led the team through a record breaking run. In 1912-13, as shown above, they won three cups under his captaincy. Harold is visible in the centre. Other notables pictured in the team are stand-off half Jim Davies, Billy Kitchen and Stanley Moorhouse, another local lad.